Konbit

Konbit

Sony Ton-Aime

Carnegie Mellon University Press
Pittsburgh 2026

Acknowledgments

Thank you to the editors of the publications where the following poems originally appeared, some in a slightly altered form:

Artful Dodge: "The Seer Sits on the Ground on the Eve the Bois Caïman Ceremony"
Consequence Forum: "The Seer Foresees Frantz Fanon on the Eve of the Bois Caïman Ceremony"
Dunes Review: "Braided"
The Idaho Review: "Death on the Eve of the Bois Caïman Ceremony," "Hope on the Eve of the Bois Caïman Ceremony," "The Seer Muses Over Toussaint Louverture on the Eve of the Bois Caïman Ceremony," and "Pidgin—Nation"
The Oakland Review: "Konbit" and "Vanishing Torso"

"To Be Young on the Eve of the Bois Caïman Ceremony" is featured in the anthology, *Dear Human at the Edge of Time*, edited by Luisa A. Igloria, Aileen Cassinetto, and Jeremy S. Hoffman, from Paloma Press, 2023.

A version of "The Circle Closes on the Day of the Bois Caïman Ceremony" appeared on the website of Kent State University.

Book design by Connie Amoroso

Library of Congress Control Number 2025938869
ISBN 978-0-88748-726-2

Printed and bound in the United States of America

10 9 8 7 6 5 4 3 2 1

Contents

Part I

Part II

Part III

Part I

On the Eve of the Bois Caïman
Our Present Time
Passive Time

The Seer Sits on the Ground on the Eve of the Bois Caïman Ceremony

Weary traveler, if upon this ground
you stumble some two hundred years later,
and if you are of the kind, make a libation.
Not that this land is sacred. No. No gods
have roamed it, nor have demons. But men
have and so have women, cursed and blessed,
not unlike you. If their blood in your veins
does not run, do not blaspheme their deaths.
No sacrifice is ever wasted, for on the other
side of the world someone is dying of thirst.
The water you pour and the tree you mend
will one day provide shade to another soul.
So, as you rest and breathe here, know
someone could have been saved.

The Seer Foresees the Following Events on the Eve of the Bois Caïman Ceremony

a broken sonnet

Three hundred years of pain dropped in the night's rain,
from the first boat anchored to the last broken chain.
Tonight, we walk—no, run—over their profit-maker,
their plantations, their survival, our body-grinder.
Machetes, rusty bayonets, torches in hands
marching forward, snaking around the wasted land.
Hear the swift sound of our intent winged feet
hovering over the ground as the tanbou skips beats.
This is nature at work. A knot tied for too long
calcifies and hardens, but after a while, breaks
under stress and habits of the mind rebelling
against idleness of the body; for, in constant danger
the slave, too, can still find comfort.

Boukman Says Goodbye to His Master on the Eve of the Bois Caïman Ceremony

after Tim Seibles

And you, my torturer, here in this hot room,
teach me your tough love. Oh, how I cry.
Do not mourn me when my head is pruned to bloom,
for the dead will return with fire in its eyes.
Do not mourn my departure from your room.
Sir, you had it coming your whole life. You
flogged, flogged my mother's back till it bled.
Do not mourn my hands in your doom.
Though men like you I shall order to kill,
you, sir, my rebirth will see.
Good men, so many, you have put to sword
for no reason but wanting to reach old age:
do not mourn their fate, for in death they bloom.
Evil men you called them, because they refused
to accept théir doom, their want of repose, of freedom,
sweep your rooms, genuflect and kiss your broom.
Do not mourn my departure from your room.
Teach me now your tough love, I rebel.
Flogged, flogged my mother's back till it bled.

The Seer Predicts Boukman's Death on the Eve of the Bois Caïman Ceremony

You, who brought the sun and showed us its light,
whose voice moved our bodies like the sea and
turned their fire into roaring thunders, listen well.
You, bodiless and motionless cloud, watch over us.
Their god demanded crimes, and they delivered.
Now, show us what good deeds mean. O you,
severed head, a warning on display. What does
the lord ask of us now that your arms are gone?
O you, beautiful phantom torso, ball of caged words,
direct our hands and guide us away from theirs.
Feed the voice of liberty unto us. And forgive
them for they know not the pit they have dug.
This all will come to pass on Assumption Day;
your soul will rise up as you become a savage.

Toussaint Helps His Master Flee on the Eve of the Bois Caïman Ceremony

a broken-bodied ballade

My father was King Gaou Guinou of Allada,
before he became king-prisoner of his brother.
My mother, herself captive, reared me in Breda.
Despite her pained life, she never once shuddered
in the face of fear or the absence of a man—my father—
who himself was traded before air filled my lungs,
before my eyes opened and saw the world shattered
by a master I loved and who loved my body.

A body I loved and a master who loved me
equally restrained and enslaved to one another.
Small and weak in stature, not unlike a flimsy
stick, this body the Lord gave me pleased Master.
And Master in turn groomed it into a fighting rooster,
a handler, healer, coachman, watcher of Breda,
but a slave I remained, toiling next to better
men and women who called me *bâton-fatras.*

Bâton-Fatras they called me, shame of Allada.
Stout yet small bodied for a good horse driver,
I dazzled as they laughed, stubborn as a Capois.
Pierre-Baptiste Simon, the purveyor, my godfather
a lover of good speech who hated the sugar crusher,
judged it wise to teach me grammar as a contingency.
He trained my mouth and my soul, yet still I uttered
thanks to a master and a God who loved me.

And me who loved and thanked Master and God
whose children will grow free and resentful
of my action and fealty. Here I stand as I present
myself in your broken tongue—progeniture.

A Mother Sends Her Son Off
on the Eve of the Bois Caïman Ceremony

If their language
you must speak,
son, make it yours.
By that, I mean
make it roll on
your tongue as you do
in the kitchen.
The R like a pin
on wet sticky flour.
The U like an oven,
an open I teeth out
both a grateful smile
and a caged tiger.
In their ears your S
should be hooves hitting
cobblestones,
but know unlike their horses,
you cannot tame souls.
When you chew on good food,
curl your E around your lips.
May it not be a reflection
of anything, less of you.
May it catch their hands midair.

The Rain on the Eve of the Bois Caïman Ceremony

Outside, the rain like an importune guest comes knocking,
the flowers fold on themselves and the earth unfurls and filters
its gift through the slats under our sheets into our nostrils.
Predictably, the thunder follows the zigzag of interspersed lightnings,
and in between, a muffled chant of drops hit the palm thatches.
Tutu, the dog, shakes and leans on the bed's right hind leg
with his eyes peering up under his ears at each flash. In the garden,
green snakes slither under dead alocasia leaves by the chicken coop.
The night sky, in a jolly mood, dances, dark and deaf to the calls below.
Beauty abounds in disaster, we know. The world dies and our eyes
are cast down. The white god on his throne shines like a bone.
A whip awaits—after a Sunday spent in the arms of a husband—
on a profitable plantation, on borrowed time, on good returns.
The best comes last. And nothing is sweeter than death.

A Mistress in Bed with Her Husband on the Eve of the Bois Caïman Ceremony

His suppled hands cup my face, and my cheeks on fire
move up for a kiss. His belly tightens and my thighs sigh

wet and hungry. I close onto him. The vigor of his thrusts,
the smell of fresh absinthe from Fatiman's cabin emitting

from his pale soft skin is both sickening and thrilling.
Plantation work, he calls it. Cliché yet practical.

Flesh against flesh, throbbing absent of pleasure. There
is a math to it. When body is insurance and survival,

a woman can only watch her man's daughter busying
in the kitchen, and wonder how nature can bestow upon

a wretched girl such beautiful eyes, so blue, so foreign.
As his breath shortens and his cadence fluctuates,

the sign he is approaching his end and my beginning,
my inside explodes and the fire spreads from my head

down my esophagus to my gut and through him. There,
as he lost himself in a hiccup, Fatiman's face leans

over the spear and his throat opens in bloody jubilation.

Fatiman Contemplates the Knife on the Eve of the Bois Caïman Ceremony

after Pierre Corneille

blood-tinted blade
rusted yet never dull
prayer in waiting
always out of reach
you so many times
have failed me
you for far too long
have been hidden
your time has come
leave your sheath
stop digging into
this worn-out flesh
and find more worthy cause
you for too long
have seen my pain
and chose peace
peace in such time
is mutiny
you should know

Fatiman's Parents Chide the Child on the Eve of the Bois Caïman Ceremony

dissociative sonnets after Tyehimba Jess

It could have been worse if you'd ask me. Always.
Look at your legs—stiff, intact, and attached to your hips.
Yes, sometimes they are opened by hands other than yours, but it
could have been worse. My master, your master's father, spread
mine, and when they ran from him, he chopped one. The day of your birth
the dog dug the big bone out behind the hut and brought it in its mouth
to my bed. You giggled and ran your fingers on its smooth knuckles,
but it could have been worse. I could have lost both. There is always
a universe where things could have gone twice as bad. In it, you could
have been worse; white and married with only rage and a whip to bring
you life's delights. Has my love not been enough of a consolation
that you need your body to be freed from the good Lord's control? Oh,
uppity girl! Oh, calamity's sister, have I not traced in your palm the ancestors'
lineage? Have our roots withered and dried up so fast under your feet?

One rare, unburdened Sunday, my father scratched his feet,
furrowed his brows before letting out a sigh. "Your ancestors,"
he told me, his voice a rumbling of shame and short control, "Oh,
girl, you know not fighting. You think death is your only consolation?
Under your tongue, a rebellion of words forged in secret, to bring
about change. A stand to subterfuge. A language that could
escape the misery of toiling, a bent back that seems always
to say, we can still laugh at the devil up to when his knuckles
hit our jaws. "We wound the whip sound from our mouths
and turned the ashes of words into life before your birth.
This is your legacy, girl. This is revolution! Twice opened
and still unbroken. It could have been worse, if you'd ask me, but it
is not. You know why? We gave you words heavier than hips,
because you can speak without master knowing. Remember that. Always."

The Seer Foresees Frantz Fanon on the Eve of the Bois Caïman Ceremony

A
hoe
loosed
on one's
right shoulder
is both comfort and
a weapon depending on
what road one chooses to take.
A man, when stripped of his humanity
& beaten by another who calls himself master,
goes home with bruises to nurse or avenge depending
who he finds waiting. Chay lou sòti sou tèt, li tonbe sou zepòl.
At the neck of it a woman sat, a shingle
holding two two-by-fours between three slats,
a thatch roof threating to cave in.
There, the windows are shut, and dense
air hovers over thin/black/naked bodies.
This here is a house built on water for the sole purpose of continuity.
Let's rebuild it, they say, hands enjoined
behind the man as he reports on their fate.
Look at them, he says, and we look
at the camera. They can't help themselves.
The boy opens his mouth, and his mother
joins in, they sing a song and the feed cuts. Nou sove peyi n
they sing over and over until the man eats his tongue.
The camera turns back on as the man bleeds,
the boy and his mother stop,
& men in uniform,
the witnesses
come
get
it.

Toussaint Justifies Saving His Master on the Eve of the Bois Caïman Ceremony

Indeed, I did.

Death on the Eve of the Bois Caïman Ceremony

The boy's lungs gave up under life's insouciance.
We stood in line to wash him and give him his two wails
as his mother made coffee behind the shack, & the choir
sang as the father and the other son made the coffin.
This cannot be it, we told the boy lying on the cot. His eyes
turning inside now, to a better world. Life could not be
just toiling and failing. There must be something else.
So, we laughed and danced after our wailing. For, who
among us could say they were better off than the boy?
This is death. This is jouissance. This is free time.
Time to plot. Time to pull the rug. Boukman's time.
He came with his machete dangling by his waist, his face
the shadow of gods, said, Tonight the world dies with us!
Over our shouts and wails, we heard dawn breaking.

Hope on the Eve of the Bois Caïman Ceremony

is what we call a version of: a feeling with no name,
a proxy. The word existed, of course, so was the world.
What was lost has been in our palms all along, vice versa.
Generations of fathers' and mothers' bodies scraping on
boat underbellies. Names erased and trees decimated.
Memory of home washed clean in the dark. Murmur
of syllables deprived language of its meanings. After
years of sameness, of deception and deprivation,
one can only look at the blank canvas and behold
the reflection of the past, the only certainty. Life
is found in the good book we can read but hear
Moses had his God, and we have the afterlife,
blazing brighter than any burning bush
and much more alive, too, we're told.

Birthday on the Eve of the Bois Caïman Ceremony

Best wishes for the new day, for
the new hour, minute, and second.
Here, life is counted by breaths.
As we dry our eyes,
a man grieves
a daughter eaten
by a big-bellied mouth.
It had swallowed generations
before her. Yet,
today you dance.
We save our breaths,
and remember
there are mothers
crying for their youths
and daughters dreaming
of a changed world
on your birthday, child.

Pidgin—Nation

If defiance is the point, then yes.
        Taut tongue twister ties in meanings.
    A nod is not a nod if the left eye shifts. Twice,
if the lips touch and teeth are shown short after,
        we have a no. It is revolution work
not a master-slave understanding.

Here is Boukman. A word that sticks
in between mouth and unlit pipe. Letters,
weighted, dusted, and cleaned to the bone.
Boukman is djanm: *adj.* from French jambe,
meaning leg. If Boukman stands up, then
he is brave. Per edict, running means
losing a leg and yet, here he stands.

His voice as hoarse as the horse he
hops on, asking that we touye limyè a
as he crouches down. Touye: *v.* from tuer,
meaning to kill. To kill the lights in one's eyes
is to blind us all, sa nou *tout ye*, he says.
At the end of the road, "bout" that is,
someone whose face is vaguely familiar
will pronounce in broken Creole,

Bondié ki fait soleil, qui clairé nous en haut.

Here precision is key, for we know God.
In the back pew, we see His back,
neck showing under sweaty blond locs
warning of latches and cat hauling. No.

For us, God should be bon, meaning good.
And that is the trick: to name one's God,
and the Devil worshipers respond.

At last, sound and silence are made one:
hints bursting out of nothing, mirror
dazzling the mind, silence wilding like
gunpowder, all to say the obvious,
a human is a human and no one knows
where a word's leg ends or begins.

On the Eve of the Bois Caïman Ceremony God Appears

in the form of my father's laughter, round,
dark, suppled, and sore like a crow midair.
In his Sunday best, his smile whiter than
his shirt, yet yellow under the vest. The shaft
in his right hand grazes his left calf.
I open my eyes, and here he still stands, grinning.
That's my pop alright. I hear his thoughts,
his voice, my conscience. The echo of work
and obedience. My father was no savage.
This poem is conscious of that, even when
it can never trace his face, the way his eyes
flushed the pain down his cheeks, or the way
his lips quivered and shook with delight, or
the way God can never know loss or death.

Fatiman Spells Out Her Name to Secure the Pig on the Eve of the Bois Caïman Ceremony

Ceremony stands, though my name should suffice.
Empty-handed, yet unblushingly, I come to you,
countryfolks and gods of the high land. Your hands,
illicit and knowing, abet our endeavor. Will you
leave behind all your life's possessions, all you
earned, all in this one pig that I demand of you?

Faithful sister, will you share this cup with us
at the risk of being fooled once more? I ask you
time and time again to forfeit your future and
impawn your children's safety, their trust in you.
Make the bet and jump into history's darkness
answer fate's call, ret vijilan epi met fanm sou nou
nan san kochon aswè a, we will map our deaths.

The Seer Muses Over Toussaint Louverture on the Eve of the Bois Caïman Ceremony

This Toussaint is trouble, I tell you that for nothing.
A freed man in this land is a danger, even if his skin
glistens in the sun and his palms are dark and rugged.
His smart, hard work, his dedication, his success, all
will be seen by the world over, and the masters. He will
be called to lead, a leader of our time. A pedestal will
be placed under his small legs, and just when we think
we can take it no more, we will think of him and say
to ourselves, "if only we had worked hard, we too,
could be Toussaint." He will then smack his chest,
spit on the ground, and say to himself, "I have done it,
I have avenged my people." The shackles on our feet
then will sing for another day, and our masters will
put on their best hats on their way to church.

To Be Young on the Eve of the Bois Caïman Ceremony

Fatiman, come and see.
The last mapou has fallen.
The last giant is conquered.
They have done it, zanmi m.
Their small hands have crushed life.
Look at us on the TV,
the angles of our feet,
our extended bellies.
Look into the camera, tifi.
All around us, all our eyes can see
are sugar canes and white spires;
man-made pillars of life.
Behold! The same hands that broke our backs
have come for the earth.
Vini m di w.
Look how much care and
attention they put into slicing open
the land and carving the map.
Look here, the zigzag line
that follows up north ends in darkness.
Fatiman dear, why are your hands red?

Making Love on the Eve of the Bois Caïman Ceremony

The smoothness of her black skin,
the white lines on his elbow:
such beauty cannot be spoiled.
Their lips touch as their faces
seemed miles apart. Even here
in a such private act, there can
be no full abandonment.
The eyes are ever watching. Remember.
The ears are ever closing in. Remember.
The almost-violent violet
of her gum under her white pearls,
he knew but could not see.
The urchins' giggles barely covered
her moans. Around them,
bodies in slumber snored, sniffed
dry sweat under their armpits.
This, too, could be work, they knew
if the eyes watching were blue.

The Seer Cannot Say What Happened on the Eve of the Bois Caïman Ceremony

First, the dog never asked to be trained
to chase and chomp hands or legs. Nor were
the taste and smell of Black bodies ever
of interest to him when he was a good boy.
Good Boy we called him as he licked
our bloody fingers, the knife at his throat.

Second, his master on the bed. Peaceful.
We forgot not they were once babies.
There is no humanity in taking back
one's humanity. The wild is made wild
& even in its tamest position, the lion
hunts in the prey's mind. The dog's master
died with his tongue lolling out.

Third, because we always come last.
Slowly we lost our seeing and hearing so
that only rage is left,
and dreams and their haunting.
So many problems we've solved in that place.

Part II

On the Day of the Bois Caïman
Our Present Time
Revolution Time

On the Day of the Bois Caïman Ceremony

the moon stays long past noon.
the sun shines on the outside
and no one says shh.
silence swings over the valley
and the rooster's beak, quiet drum.

a day starts and new ideas
go to sleep with open eyes.
Boukman wakes up
and sits by the well.
the hero is nowhere
to be found again.

the savior will not come
during our time, not before
the good word reaches the edges
of the Earth, but behind
the horizon is horizon.
a master has an heir,
and a spade is replaceable.

on the day the circle breaks,
Fatiman watches
as the land opens
and the people stand.
no horsemen come,
no thunder claps.
there, they raise their hands
and light the torches.

A Business Lesson on the Day of the Bois Caïman Ceremony

Plainly put, the seer cannot write, so
a prophet is needed, a middleman.

The soothsayer counts his earnings,
the dirt under his fingers is still wet, and

the smell of blood reeks the soil, thinks,
that, minus the seer's take, is profit;

pro—mine, *fit*—ness, the other's
presence, personal expenses,

plus a new pen, a wag of paper are
cost of goods, of doing business.

The seer's message is raw materials
to flesh out the mumbling, the medium.

The time spent learning to write and listen,
is an investment worth its return.

***

the seer's stake is benefis,
benefit, *bene facere,* to do good in

a new language is to take the self
out, to bring in the community.

The land that soaks the blood &
sweat pro bono, never asks what's

in it, for it is what you receive,
simple as that, gratis = benefis.

For the bien-être of others, we
toil together, we sow in tandem,

eat only what we need or
is offered. Lofty words but

a tongue made to conquer
the world cannot mend it.

To Be Optimistic in a Dying World

The earth is dying,
by that, I mean we are.
We use our hands &
the roses wither,
the mud expands.
Even the water is lonely,
always looking for its way
to the ocean. The future
gasps for air, chokes
on blindness and greed.

This is the time &
place for hope, so
we lie. We are humans,
beasts of dreams &
of wishes. We keep
looking at the mud &
calling it gold, or
the possibility of it.
This is what we do;
we survive 'till we die.

There is a bridge
between here and nowhere.
Here, for example, a creek
runs witless for ages.
Perches, carps, trout &
basses fry up before they
bite the bait.

The dam collects their bones. Yet
nowhere else are the fish so lovely.
We too are lonely, but
nowhere are we dying. Yet.

The Circle Closes on the Day of the Bois Caïman Ceremony

The little Pigmy who first jumped into the Congo River
could teach de Soto a thing or two about the Mississippi.
It is the same water flowing in our hearts, through our veins,
from the River Jordan to the altar of the last Chilean priest.

The pregnant mother who breaks water accomplishes
no lesser feat than Moses before the Red Sea.
The men who went to the moon brought their mud with them;
so did the woman who leapt, legs wide open, into the volcano.

Before the Messiah met John the Baptist,
our ancestors worshiped the sun, rocks, and trees,
until one rainy October day, Massacre River ran with blood
and flesh, carrying in its mighty bed their gods

and their hope. When I was little, my momma told me
the future is a snake swallowing its tail. My daddy said
it was a dog sucking on his own dick, that we ought to have
another Gandhi, another Einstein, King, Kennedy,
and, no doubt, another Adolf. Life will continue,
swallowing its circle.

Kinanm vs. Pam on the Day of the Bois Caïman Ceremony

Below the mountains where evil dwells, good folks
with gold gleaming in their eyes lose their heads,
believe they too can own pour and make it pam.
Wait and see, they say, we will have our own hands.

Once these chains fall and we climb the rungs,
the servants will serve us tea under the mapou, too.

In the woods where darkness does it best, the hands
who escaped the masters' farms cut their tongues and
sewed kinanm in their stead. Pour was never theirs
and never will be. Their eyes are wide open.

None of this means to make sense, the life they live.
Power only eats arts. Creativity is for the oppressed.
For every Pierre Nicolas Mallet Bon Blanc, there are
waiting in the shadows, ten Jean-Baptiste Conzés.

On the farms, the heavy tongues sip their rum as
the hands, always the hands, cut and refine the cane.
Each fell cane brings the end nearer, fire and water
edging ever closer as the soil loses ground and grip.

Attending a Wake on the Day of the Bois Caïman Ceremony

The bird perched on the lone branch,
poking at the window, plucked its wings,
and raindrops glided over its feathers.
The boy, naked under the eaves, no older
than the bird in dog years, and yet
the world would end for him before
the rain was over, and the bird's tweet
was a somber funeral procession for
its kin choked on dark smoke that he
mistook for a mating call, a renewal
of life, another start for a world
where the boy's father's truck used
less or braked faster than the boy
could jump and the white light flashed
slower than he could catch his breath
before asthma caught him by the creek.
The end, like a circle, has come
in many forms depending on who
you ask, if you ask me.

In the '80s the U.S. Destroyed Haiti's Rice Culture

a mélange

There is white rice on the man's plate.
Black beans-saffron-mango simmers,
rumors of dyed apron, gusto fan
the aroma of backdoor deals, a country
on its knees with promise of a full belly.
That thyme in the '80s rosemary, oregano,
fried plantains from the U.S. charred griot
sprinkled with pikliz destroyed our palates
so that Haiti's charcoal dried apricot and
jasmine rice become an imported culture
of fine grains free of pebbles.

The Seer Foresees Jacques Stephen Alexis on the Eve of the Bois Caïman Ceremony

Compère Général Soleil had a stain on his collar
the day he stood next to El Comandante.
Twelve men waited in the boat, big enough
to cradle their joy, certain to see the maternal shores

before the sun came up. Romancero aux Étoiles
felt a twinge on her left breast and she knew.
At Port-au-Prince Bay, a doctor was waiting,
eraser in hand, the final chapter is a draft.

The world told him that fingers were mightier
than guns. His mother asked him to cut them.
In Berlin, a psychic read a guillotine in his palms.

He lost a bet in Prague. The sharks confessed during
their feast that the words tasted sour. On the TV,
black and white, Papa Doc recited them aloud.

A Mistress in Bed with Her Mistress on the Eve of the Bois Caïman Ceremony

My mistress called me Mistress in bed
in the hut away from master's house. Her
scent is with me still. The raging fire growing
in intensity as we ran toward the sea, our last
goodbye. The tears we shed were not for her
dead husband. I killed him. My hand bloody
and just. She understood, she told me. We are
free now. Freedom in an empire, misnomer.
Only the pariahs are redeemed; the others,
accomplices. I am one of them. Possessing
an oppressed mistress from her possessive
master. Curtain closed, standing ovation.

The Seer Addresses the Poet on the Day of the Bois Caïman Ceremony

Look at you, digging in the past and thinking
you're it. You ain't. How can people let
this happen? You asked, as if Palestine
was not once a country and Joe is not rotting
in Congo. Not the country. The box down
in Louisiana. This evidence, to be seen,
requires open eyes. Your revolution, dear,
these words will not amount to a thing
if they fail to make their targets rich.
Brother Cohen in the future told you
what everybody knows, the crack where
the light gets in is in your heart.

Inheritance

The male hooded warbler pairs, once it accepts
its female neighbor's eggs, together shares
the work the Creator forbad in Its book,
rearing fledglings to fly away from its nest.

One Sunday, I stopped chasing my father
and fitted myself inside his red cloak.
I walked into a church, changed my socks,
and married the second woman in the confessional.

I stood in front of a mirror before I went to the brothel
and saw a man; a real beast ready to face the pack
with his bald head, a thin well-groomed mustache
with lines tracing the void felt for too many years.

The presence of his absence suffocated every memory
from First Communion to high school graduation,
except for that Sunday when the smile tattooed his lips
and I stood over his closed black box staring back.

Puppies tell their mothers when they grow up,
they will be wolves. They learn only to wag their tails
and be good. A boy is not a boy when his first knowledge
is the heaviness of his skin. At fourteen, a man knows that.

History-less

We are born with our eyes full grown,
with little plum fingers folded on themselves,
pear-shaped lips, and our heads. Yes, our heads,
hairless, bulbous, jelly moving on palms.
She found a monkey and a woman in theory.
Half Y, half X with a contradiction for body,
undeveloped nipples, brassy voice, hard knuckles,
and wide hips. We are born with features. Yet
LaWomann, formless with two gourds for breasts,
and an insatiable emperor penguin vase,
adopts unattended chicks. There are always
vagrant babies if you turn a mother invisible,
and an apt euphemism for abandonment.

Rotten

The falling dance of a fruit from a tree
doesn't tell us about its stem's putrescence.
When we pray for rain, we don't ask for
the death of the sun. It just happens.

Disciplining the body, i.e., making it white: as white
as a yellow sun, a ripe mango, or an object so far
abstract you can don it like a shield, a belt
to tie yourself into the Abrahamic genealogy.

For example: Christ once answered her prayers
while tugging at his blond locs, crouching
by a yellow shrub as he munched on fiddleheads.
Yet at the sight of the smallest nascent dark locs,
LaWomann reaches for the scissors. Haitian locs,
she calls them. She is a New World Christian
armed with a killer smile sculpted in shock.

After all, how could she survive all the hatred she cages
inside her belly if she didn't believe one can expiate
darkness by pressing nose and scrubbing skin?
For babies do come and go, but scars are eternal.
Her mother did it. Her mother's mother initiated it. And
her brother died fighting it just to be remembered
as a big nosed charcoal horsehead pagan.

Matriphagy

Twelve years later, when her son learned
of postpartum depression, LaWomann
smiled and raised her hands up to the sky.
I am a mother spider!

When she lost her Calypso body to a Medusa head,
she knew the doctors were a lost cause.
Instead, she went to the houngan who tied her down
to beat the devil out of her.
Each bite of the belt felt like a need for nutrients
on every inch of her back, her breasts, her ribs, and her thighs
unleashing wild peonies on purple flesh.

The devil, it seemed, is in her exposed derrières.
For when he felt them, his grin turned into a wide smile.
And the more she sobbed,
the more impertinently his fingers foraged
for unhatched eggs.

Aid Staff Would Pay More

actually, more than five times a local could.
With less than $2 a day and five children to feed,
not time, nor moral stand, nor erectile dysfunction,
nor religious dread, nor statutory laws would stop him.
I have amassed enough of his kind in my river delta to carve
my place in this street, in this world. Long ago, I learned
the bluer the logo on the SUV, the more likely
a gun can be pulled, or anal can be requested.
The night opens my legs with large, white hands
that secure tomorrow. Milk is expected when an ox
enters a farm but so is manure. For when the earth rumbled
with its mouth wide open and swallowed the future,
passing cars in unlit corridors colored my daughter's dream
in myriad shades of translucent green.

Vanishing Torso

after Rainer Maria Rilke

Imagine that I had indeed changed my life.
That I had started pushing up and down,
and my belly had become flatter, and my sides
more oblong, that I hadn't lacked the aristocratic grace
of a young man, that my back muscles could sprout out
at the will of my fingers, that Ardi and Lucy had run through
un-bumpy roads, that we could fill the gap
between our opposable thumbs, that age indeed was just a number,
and names were clocks lost in oblivion.
What would be left of Michelangelo, or the teste divine boys
with their extensive flowers of youth, or the one who cried
when she laughed that we-all-can-see laugh, or the man who
hid in the gym bathroom, or the girl who wore an extra bra?
It all makes me wonder if David ever was.

On the Massacre River Bridge on the Day of the Bois Caïman Ceremony

The woman who pees standing
has fire between her legs. Beautiful
rusty streams, metal hitting tortoise-
shell, iron cutting iron. Nothing less.
She travels miles with feet in the air,
elbows digging into ribs, lifting both
heavy hips and the baggage she carries.
With five mouths to feed, no time to pick
up lost shoes. The good lord must sweep
thorny streets or else she would offer
a little blood sacrifice again.

1994

The sound of my father's hammer
would wake me early in the morning.
The attic, too small to contain the cry
of the angels under his arms, would
let it filter into my room, my ears, my belly,
as if I were the sun he'd conjure to rise.
I'd start on the piano the only tune
I knew, and he would hum
the same song over and over,
willing courage in me with each strike.

***

The year I first saw my skin color,
the wind of the choppers
blew my friend's toothbrush away
over our giggles. We ran toward
the men with their long black flowers
pointing at us. Our smiles disarmed their fear
and covered their captain's order.
They became conductors with tulips
for batons, and we danced. We lowered
our backs, tightened our behinds,
and moved our shoulders and heads
in opposite directions, just like the chimps
they thought us to be. We kept executing,
kept smiling. Soldiers can't shoot glee.

***

LaWomann is made of important griefs.
Apollinaire stole her kinky hair and
replaced it with blonde weaves. Verlaine
took her sun, her coconut tree, and her beach;
gave her snow and a sense of second class in return.
Baudelaire gave her a big bottom, a creole complex.
Hugo talked of violence like he knew what raising
three kids on his own meant. Her son's heart
they conquered with words he had to turn
his tongue into a viper to pronounce.
L'hiver a couvert la terre d'un tapis blanc.
He has yet to learn Je t'aime in a language not alien to her.

***

FDA announced patient zero!
Guantanamo, declared HIV prison camp!
Haitians can no longer save
their frères de sang! Still now,
my cousin can't come out. The clock
is sure to make its round. Devastation
calls for pity, pity for fatigue, fatigue
for forgetfulness, and forgetfulness
for devastation.

***

This we took!
In exchange for our unpaid,
unacknowledged labor, our bare backs,

centuries of negation, your wealth, privileges,
your freedom, flagellations,
work in the scorching sun,
chains, rape, cat-hauling, branding,
birth of a nation, Christianity,
planking, imperialism,
Emmett Till, George Stinney
marginalization, the ghettos,
the crack epidemic:
all, we sacrificed for one word.

***

Long after he passed,
I would accompany the thrumming of the choppers
with the same tune, and they would wait
for the last note before they started shooting.
The day they took him, I asked
for music, and they gave me colors purple, red
on the street, like carnival's masks.
I asked for a boy, they gave me a burden
of dance, and of remembrance.

Braided

With each tangling of the comb in an ungreased shrub of hair, my sister let out a groan, and mother, annoyed, yelled, Stop moving, girl! The teeth of the rake hitting her bare shoulders were soon covered by the French songs dad put on to ease him back to sleep. Affaire de Femmes. The first time my mother shaved my head, she mapped the middle passage routes so artfully, you would not believe it was her ancestors who jumped off the ships. Her Van Gogh's fingers cat-hauling on my head numbed the veins such that I could barely feel the hydroxyl. It wasn't that her classmates called her horsehead or landed origami boats on her hairless skull. The day her dead cuticles touched the hot comb, she learned you could not kill what was already dead, that you needed to look further to know who you were, past your mother's oval pores, in the shaking of Miss Universe's mane. She learned straight hair does not make you less of a negress. You can still be called ratchet in your graduation gown.

Konbit

The women lead the way with their skirts tied up their bellies, stomping the ground, shaking big buttocks. Fifty choppers thrumming in the air, the hoes of the men lost their sound under the rumbling of the elder's chant. In the clamor, LaWomann's voice comes on uninvited:

Samba he, samba he, samba he

Samba comes tambou in hands a little oilier than his front. Drunk. The voice stammers, a hammer hitting cardboard. Nothing left here except for an urge. Creature of habit, he sticks his tongue out when he approaches the boys. The girls look him down, witches of another time. LaWomann invigorates delicate men:

Samba he, samba he, samba he

Men with asthma complain too much, live on the communion of brotherhood. Stumps begging for flowers on dry soil. That morning, one rooster forgot to crow and a man lost his ax. There are pebbles in his rice. LaWomann crunches her pillows under her armpits, lowers her voice, begs to differ, and whispers:

Samba he, samba he, samba he

The children fill the holes with handfuls of corn. It is life. Men dig holes, children occupy them, and women mend the world. One, two, three, tchoupth. They stop the dance when the drums start their rolling. Bellies gurgling calling out for intermission, she goes:

To a Son on His Fourteenth Birthday

If we must start somewhere, let it be with death. But before that, we will live. We will do it well, by that I mean we will play our role, pretending. For peace, you will be sent to meet a boy no older than yourself, and you'll end his road where yours should start, unpleasant and shoeless. For love, don't think. Time is precious. Smile when she leaves. Give her gifts to the sitting doctor in one of your Thursday meetings. For God, trust in your doubts. Drop on your knees when you are too sure. Speak when it is necessary, and sit down when you're tired. For politics—not that I know much but—I have seen monkeys with checkbooks do better. For power, a man can walk into the supreme court and lay his Long John Silver on the bench without losing his dignity when it comes to marriage. For race, nature decided you had to wear your crime in your eyes, hair, and fingers. For death, live in the smallest details.

The Charcoal Maker

That morning, he died for good once again.
He took his ax and machete down the hill
headed to the last maple tree,
the big one with ravens for leaves.

The sun was chasing the breeze
and the rooster that does not sing.
The maker had stopped singing long ago.
He wondered if his arms will not be soon silent, too.

The earth has become ingrate, deaf to his frail labor,
the seeds shied away from the moon and rain, last
it came, brought flood just before harvest.
No cow's desolation could lead water back to the creek.

The dust in the field welcomed him with their brown looks
as if their thirst was his fault and cutting the trees was not vital.
Looking around, he knew death will never come like this again.

Asile

". . . let us remember the baby they were
as their parents gathered them up in their arms . . ."
—Hannah Stephenson

Considering the flood and the tragedy that followed:

considering he could not bear his children's sight anymore,
considering he did not have enough in his account for a visa.
~~Strike that~~.
Considering he did not even have an account,
considering a visa cost more than his house.
Considering a place in a boat allowed him to keep his kidneys.
Considering his luck when he evaded the coast guards.
Considering his first job at Popeyes, his boss firing him
when he learned how to pronounce dignity.
Considering he later he took on carpentry,
considering you caught him on his way to work at 7 p.m.
when you heard his accent,
considering he is a criminal daring to cross borders.
But before that,
considering his wife is about to give birth. And before that his mother
once was about to give birth to her only boy.
Considering he is no stranger to violence.
~~Strike that~~.
Considering survival of the fittest
is more than just violence.
Considering his only crime was trying to survive
the survival of our doubt.
Considering he is a human,
considering no one is hurt except his ego.

Considering by bringing him here,
you assume responsibility for him and his family.
Considering a law can be criminal.

And consider for a second
this is the only way I know my father.

Ice

The man who took her boy shared her skin,
her hair, and her tongue. No tengas miedo.
While his hands closed on his little shoulders,
she saw the moon shining over Rosenstrasse,
the women who went before her each morning
yelling, Gib uns unsere Männer. Their men, they took.
The shame of their impure love, they carried.
Unlike her, they did not have to ride La Bestia
from Tegucigalpa to Texas, cross two borders,
to lose a son to an icebox.
The man who took her boy shared her blood,
her historia, and her route. No, his father did.
There are other mothers.

Perejil

On October 3, 1937, one word killed twenty-five thousand.
Two lovers were caught in the act;
bayonets pierced her belly
while he came in blood and fear.

Bodies floated in the river like crumpled leaves.
The fall matched their contrast perfectly.
The babies thrown into empty spaces giggled for
a second, before they met the end of a spear.

In San Juan, the fish cried blood,
their comrades weaving between corpses.
The frogs leapt at the shores of the river—
they could not stomach the eyes of the dead.

Cleanse the borders, Rafael said.
Paint it in blood, the people chanted.
And Haitians saturated the fertilizer
for the sugarcanes they planted that morning.

Under the complicit eyes of FDR,
Rafael and Sténio shook hands and set the price.
twenty-one dollars per person on paper. Done deal.

From Dajabón to Moca, no black men stand.
Those left were piled in trucks and dumped in the sea.
Their numbers we will never know—
they were not part of the deal.

They were wasted money.

Necklacing

The way his skin popped
like dried wood, or
the tires in their ceremonial
dark smoke kept him
straight while ardent fire
puffed out of his mouth,
the way the others clapped
and cheered
at the marvel of a cheap jug
of gasoline
a handful of matches,
and the way I forced myself
to stare at LaWomann
in the corner sobbing,
as if I, too, did not point
my thumbs down.

Fear Felt Up North on the Day of the Bois Caïman Ceremony

When sleep would not come, Jefferson,
grasping the edges of his desk, wrote
to his legal wife, *Of the whites' expulsion*
from the West India Islands while people
of colour remain, I become convinced
is a dangerous fermentation.
Never was so deep a tragedy felt.

Oh, the lies, Fatiman, I tell you, the lies.
Our freedom has enough legs to carry all.
Liberation means Martha, too, will be
at the garden table, next to Sally, but
they won't be his. It means the Chinese,
the Japanese will be in. The sisters, the strippers,
the felons will be let in. So will be
the mothers and brothers inside.
Legs, arms, brains refuse to rot.

Lift EVERY voice, we say. Ask Castaine and Lachaise.
While you're at it, ask Cher and Ms. Patton,
they too are invited to the barbecue.

The Good Master Explains Things on the Day of the Bois Caïman Ceremony

things were different then
our present can't explain then
then it was what everyone did
those who ran away then
we amputated and cut their tongues
then they were silent/unpeopled

true things were different
like now, things are different
our children will say so we hope
those silent and unpeopled
are not our doing for all who
have eyes can now see it

those who will run away
or wag their tongues will make
things different and everyone
will need to do the silent nod
and together we will explain
just wait a little for us
to catch up baby steps please

Part III

On the Day After the Bois Caïman
Our Children Time
Truth Time

On the Day After the Bois Caïman Ceremony, God

welcomed the faithful to heaven,
and they deposed her,
before they built their own
and after they brought from
the mines the new hands
with their feet soiled in oil
black as heart and glimmering as gold.
Let us now praise the world
we've made with each
tree planted, each trip omitted,
and each chop pock chewed.
Let the world be its own master,
to keep its secrets and fuel its
own turning around the sun.
May it be so that the impossible
known and unknown be god again
and our hands smaller and mighty
not our dwelling or our aim.
May it be so that we become
beautiful again like the faces
of our children
like young mountains.

On the Day After the Bois Caïman Ceremony

We wake up the same, and the world changes.
The wind takes on new ways of howling. Trees
uproot themselves from such anger, and the rain
is of no help, mindlessly carried roads and signs.

Inside, a man curls up next to a woman, begs
for forgiveness for only the umpteenth time.
How did he manage it, she asks, and he giggles
as her right fist meets his left side.

The girl pulls in between her father's legs. He
parts her hair and weaves them between his fingers
into short tresses. The boy sits with an open book
on his laps, drools, and snores. The uncle smokes.

The world's end the seer had promised did not come.
No one died of weakness, it was a lie.
We wanted too much.

On the Day After the Bois Caïman Ceremony, César Vellajo Spoke

Tomorrow is already gone and yesterday,
well, yesterday will wear its own green coat.
The country that never was and never will be
is now the Pearl of the Antilles.

Only the trivial should be put under serious
consideration. Everything else is delight.
Tomorrow was an insatiable animal, mouth
agape, and we are only what we are: time clocks.
After Tuesday, Monday is a lonely ocean.
And the shore is in the margins, friends.

Not everyone will be queer or Black tomorrow,
but everything else will be seamed in the same
patterns, mark my word. Only the serious
will be proven right, but it was too late, we know.

Tomorrow sat at yesterday's door and gossiped.
All night, the voices at the cemetery were silent
words written in a foreign calligraphy, with
meaning we perceived with bat ears and dog nose.
There was a reason for all this that we accepted
was never worthy of time and place.

The More Things Change on the Day After the Bois Caïman Ceremony

What is bound to happen, that we call the future, is a game your father played in his childhood. CC O BB KK 100 BC. The boys laughed and choked, and choked and laughed. A room dense in fume. What did they know? Nothing you don't. The scourge goes on and no time to gauge the scope of its truth. All dead are terrorists. Debate me, you twit. Have you seen the tattoo like a little black hole in his forehead? By the time you're home, he will be long gone. The lord knows how sorrow grows.

The Earth Elegy on the Day After the Bois Caïman Ceremony

Terre, dear, your name came up again.
Beyond the years and remembrance,
five letters are what's left.
Your face has faded, its features lost,
its bones long gone, returned to dust.
In my fifth-grade notebook, the poem
is written in past tense. Your eyes were
brown and your cheeks were white.
I don't know what it meant.
I stole it from a book, probably,
as I am now stealing the time we never
shared, the laughs I can't recall.
Were you ever beautiful?
It was love before the meaning of love.
It'd be true even if I were blind.
My mother said I was too young.
I did not know what age was then.
I know not what memory is now.
Terre, the scythe came too early.

Praise the Colony Built on the Day After the Bois Caïman Ceremony

A colony is a place, borderless, engulfing lives. Yet
a colony of minds, a borderless place, can heal lives.

Mars comes to mind, a soil-poisoned place. What
colony wasn't built on lies and broken lives?

On the eve of the happening lies were told and a broken
colony was the result and out came, they say, new lives.

The poet lost his name, so there could be no ghazal in
a colony. Bless those ready to lose their lives,

for even the name is ambivalent. In the new
colony, will it degrade or enhance our lives?

En un clin d'oeil

The poet, in his right mind, sees the world and says perceive.
To the woman rushing to catch the train, the world is the world,
and the eyes see what the eyes see.
She can't read, and he can't know.
Tied legs at the bottom of a tall ladder,
He never writes I love you in a poem, but says it all the time.
Shame is being conscious of time,
and words uttered are the present moment even if they last an eternity.
She catches his eyes no rounder than the dog's she shooed away
that morning. He knew.
No verse can show love like the clumsy gaze of a stranger in haste.

On the Day After the Bois Caïman Ceremony a Baby Becomes a Woman in a City that Becomes a Country then Becomes a Life

I

When a child was born in the countryside,
the umbilical cord was dried, saved, and planted
under a tree at the mother's accord. We fought
over the gods, and they lost us. Like fools, we
multiplied. On her birthday, lightning split
the tree. She grew treeless until Papa God
came shouting, *You shall be my own child, dear.*
The magic orange tree lowered and ate her fear.

She was a précoce child, impatient to open
her eyes. Her mother was on her seventh month
when her two small legs came first, the mambo
yelled, *ay, the devil eat my tongue she be not dead.*
Blood filled in her nose. A thin gel crowned
her head. To be clear, girls are never born right
or on time. Was it to be so? Would we lie to them
and let their pilgrimage to Golgotha ensure?

2

Now, babies do not come out of thin air, do they?
Before the seven months, her mother worked day
and night, spying on the moon, spotting its fullness
and avoiding laying for too long on her left breast.
There are things the Houngan cannot tell you.
When a man wants another boy out of you, he kisses
your dimples and lifts your right thigh and sighs.
But for the girl he never wants, you wind your hips.

And her mother danced hard and she opened her eyes
and she became a witch and she caught men's lies
and she swam with the silver-golden fish and naked she was
hairless in her staunched little eight-year-old and she
danced the Kokoyiko dance and offered all and more
Papa God echoed behind the men's dripping tongues
counting days and years before she's ripe enough
to stand straight and tall and tied to the stake.

3

LaWomann grew up with her parents and siblings
but happy is a tricky word to translate when
stomachs and baskets keep emptying their guts.
Shards of glass stab soft tongues. She grew up.
Damballah Oueddo fought Papa God over her, but
she chose to worship the ashy cross and hid
the star-shaped scar on her left shoulder.
Her belly danced as she looked up to the Virgin.

As her belly danced, she recited ten Ave Marias,
crossed her legs, and crossed herself with holy water.
Podyab! Little soul didn't know when Damballah claims
a girl, she becomes a pariah, and no Pater Noster,
no Gloria can save her apple from the touch of dreams.
Her mother waited for the mid-sky sun, burned her skirt
and made a circle around her bed with the ash.
Away be the evil spirit, eaters of young girls' bellies.

4

Like most women, LaWomann married the wrong man.
Not wrong in the fact that he was simply a man; for a man
he was good, a man looking too much like his old man,
an annihilator,   as people would call his kind later.
Now like any good storyteller I'll start at the beginning
before the gods left.   LaWomann was not from Benin
like most believe. She was the earth's daughter, or its mother
if you believe it to be more than just matter.

Or she made her own life that I would never
tell right or she lost her power under my tongue
or she boiled her teeth in the three-legged pot at night or
it was me who longed for her mouth to break into songs
or she was only a child or I was asking for too much
or none of this matters or we ought to flush
it all down in memory's maw or magnify what is
or is our joy comparable to what is our ply?

5

Because life was away from home and her mother
had to find it and she had to eat and because she was
a baby and she sucked on the neighbor's milk-less breasts
and because she was a hungry baby and placebo is ignorance
satiated and she kept crying and the skeptical neighbor
put three grains of salt under her tongue and because
salt is not diamond and she kept crying and because
alcohol is no melatonin for a child, she passed out.

Either life was away from home or the embargo was not
or the contraband oil she sold was for her fat mouth or
she fed her daughter on either air or salt. Either she
broke the law or she sold her mangos to the others
selling their secondhand clothes her future selves.
Either she made three trips or four depending on if
the guards were en garde or asleep. Either way
she was one of the winged, unmiraculous women.

6

Pise manman mwen fè kim, tonnè
her mother takes a piss and a well is dug
she said. Li genbe m anba zèl li kont malfektè
not all crimes can be erased with a shrug
Mwen fout grandi nan mitan gran frè ak sè
who carried her sorrows in her skin under a shrug
nan lari kote solèy pa janm touche tè
she touched the earth and puffed on her last nug.

That night, when she put her ears down on her pillows, he came through the keyhole to make an even smaller hole in her. He hit the circle of ash from her mother's burned skirt. The toes that touched the ash circle came off clean. O, how he galloped! How he yelled! Tonnè boule! In the other room, LaWomann's mother grinned. She knew iron cut iron. A lion in the sea is no king. Ogou is the only remedy for Damballah's scheme.

7

Yon famn kay stays at home and raises heads
like cattle a man will lose in a failing farm
not because she wants it, but what can be done
in the face of traditions older than headless rainbows
lost in the clouds. LaWomann's mother
did not make men men or women women.
She herself dances in between flower beds
and bamboo mats. Hips widen faster than age.

To miss a child that was never a child
exacerbates its memory, the vee between
neck and shoulders perfect for a round head.
The aimless palm hitting numb knees,
a reminder of the shape of anger at
the anger of not feeling angry taking roots
under the nails digging, scratching
the phantom of what could have been.

8

This was the time her mother started remembering.
But old age spoils memories: the first kiss, the third child,
when you brought her to the gate of the church and
took five steps away before the priest yelled, “Ma’am,
you forgot your baby,” and you hid your anger with a
faked surprise. On your way home, you kicked the priest’s
fat cat, and you thought this unwanted daughter you are holding
will never be as fat as this cat, and neither anyone you knew.

By old age, I mean try to picture a forty-six-year-old
whose life was spent on lifting big bundles of mangos,
carrying them across the river between two rows of laughing
guards betting on who could hit all her ribs before she fell.
I mean imagine giving birth to five children having never seen
a white-robed person, except for the priest who wouldn’t take
her daughter. I mean think of a body older than forty-six years, of
a winkled face that people blame on want of laughter.

9

There is death. It has always been here. Its severed
head poking out at each step: each flashing of a fist,
each sign so easy to miss, each line we scratch
along the way, each time we utter the word *life*,
death smiles. Yet, we drudge along as if those on
top, their boots were flies, as if their imprints
were not gobbling the air, and the trees could
litigate their case in the court of high ground.

Yet, there is life. It has
always been this way. Why should
we lose heart now? When LaWomann's
mother passed, she cried herself to work.
The Word man told her. Soon
they will be reunited in death and these
words gave her new breath, new life, and
she clung to it with all her teeth.

10

LaWomann's mother was no fool that woman
she none told her daughter the world was hers
no no sir she got the damn truth LaWomann did
the best you can expect from the mad world is
a son who will carry you to your last rest
and hope to never see his back through bars
she knew LaWomann she was no dummy was she
she wished for no belly of hers to carry a boy.

And he died the boy died he died like really died
as in died yesterday died cold died today died
in his bed died eternity died he died with his eyes
died left in died bright daylight died we will never know
how he died one moment he died next he died she
said he died she can't die after he died who would die
and let her die we are used to he died we live with it
she died after he died it wasn't a lie they both died.

A Word About Konbit

I was raised by a small community in the northeastern region of Haiti. My Haitian folks will get what I will say here, but for some readers, it might sound only like a metaphor. It is not. My community literally raised me. My neighbor's daughter babysat me. When I ran beyond the neighborhood's limits, it was the neighbor who walked me home because my father worked in another city. My neighbor's son taught me to ride a bicycle. Raising me was a konbit—this beautiful Haitian concept of true collectivism where neighbors take turns to help each other in everything from rearing children to harvesting the land.

The Bois Caïman ceremony, for me, was the first example of konbit in Haiti's history. In the poems in this collection, I am attempting to imagine and bring together what would give my ancestors the confidence to rise against those who held them in slavery for some 300 years.

The ceremony happened on the night of August 14,1791. It is considered the impetus of the Haitian Independence Revolution. Under the leadership of the Houngan Dutty Boukman and the Mambo Cécile Fatiman, the enslaved people held a voodoo ceremony in Bois Caïman, a city in the north of Haiti (Saint-Domingue then). There they pledged and planned a revolution, which they started ten days later by burning plantations in Cap-Haitien (Cap-Français then). They would continue the fight under different leaders and in different forms for the next twelve years until the ultimate victory on November 18, 1803, in Vertières, only some miles from Bois Caïman.

At the time, very few of the people in this collection—and in history—had members of their families or friends who were born free. Those like Toussaint Louverture (a leader of the revolution) who were able to buy their freedom spent most of their lives toiling incessantly afterward anyway. But, seeing how some of our contemporaries hold dear to the myth of pulling oneself by the bootstraps, I can imagine how enticing it might have been to my ancestors to believe that if they worked hard enough, maybe one day they too could purchase their freedom. Can you imagine what it would take for them to wake up from such a dream?

What about us?

Sony Ton-Aime

Acknowledgments

I owe thanks to too many people and institutions to be able to mention them all here. This collection is indeed a konbit, a communal work that started on August 14, 1791, at Bois Caïman, so that is where I will start. Thank you to the ancestors who inspired me and made freedom possible.

Thank you to my family for their sacrifices. To my country, Haiti, I dedicate this and everything that I do. You are worth more than we can give you.

To my friends, teachers, and editors; Maj Ragain, Seth Murray, Tahirah Walker, Caleb Gill, Ted Lyons, Hilary Plum, Edwin and Emily, Percival Everett, Victoria Chang, Shara McCallum, Scott Cunningham, Charlie, David, Jessica, Gyorgyi, everyone at the Wick Poetry Center, my NEOMFA peeps, Chautauqua Institution, and Pittsburgh Arts & Lectures.

The collection would not be possible without the good folks at Carnegie Mellon University Press. I am grateful to the best editor in the world, Jake Grefenstette; to the amazing interns, Jen Bortner, Dylan Courtney; and to the one that keeps it all going, the intrepid production manager, Connie Amoroso.

And finally, to Ying Zhao.